T0064247

The BEST GREEN BAY FOOTBALL BABY NAMES

Dr. Jon Kester

authorHOUSE®

AuthorHouse™
1663 Liberty Drive
Bloomington, IN 47403
www.authorhouse.com
Phone: 833-262-8899

Published by AuthorHouse 03/18/2021

ISBN: 978-1-6655-2032-4 (sc)
ISBN: 978-1-6655-2031-7 (e)

Library of Congress Control Number: 2021905816

Print information available on the last page.

This book is printed on acid-free paper.

Dedication

This book is dedicated to my dad, Denis. He taught me growing up how to love babies and the Green Bay Packers. This led me to become an amazing Packer fan and Dad.

Contents

Importance of Choosing A Baby Name

Naming your child may feel like one of the grueling parts of being pregnant (besides actual labor, of course). When Choosing a name be sure to think about what's important to you. Do you want something unique, traditional or somewhere in between? While this book can't choose the baby's name for you, we can give you over 100 examples of names of real live champions both on and off the field. Remember Choosing your baby's name should be one of the joys of parenting much like watching the Green Bay Packers should be one of the joys of your free time.

The way parents see the world and the lifestyle they value often determine the name they pick, according to Victoria Rodgers, author of 24/7 baby doctor. Naming your child after a champion person like many of the Packer players is the finest way to choose the name of your new bundle of joy.

Remember the name you pick holds the power to shape your child's self-esteem and their identity—and even influence how they are treated by others. There's the belief that a child's name have been proven to affect everything from self-confidence to grades in school and even their future professional success. This is where the importance of this book comes into play. It will help all parents find their child a name after a group of successful, champion, Hall of Fame, class act people. The Best place to look for these amazing role models is in Titletown, U.S.A and there professional football team.

WHY SHOULD I NAME MY BABY AFTER A PACKER?

The big question that comes up is why should I name my baby after a Green Bay Packer player and not after my Grandma Dorothy or maybe have my baby named after my favorite food like apple. Well the four main reasons are:

1) The Packer are champions in life
2) The Packers are Hall of Fame People
3) The Packers are Loyal to their community
4) The Packers are a class act

Champions

The Green Bay Packers have won more championships (13) than any other team in National Football League history.

They won their first three by league standing (1929, 1930 and 1931), and 10 since the NFL's playoff system was established in 1933,1936, 1939, 1944, 1961, 1962, 1965, 1966, 1967, 1996 and 2010). Green Bay also is the only NFL team to win three straight titles, having done it twice (1929-30-31 and 1965-66-67). (https://www.packers.com/history/championship-seasons)

In addition, the Packers won the first two Super Bowls (over Kansas City in 1966, 35-10, and over Oakland in 1967, 33-14), as well as two more recently (over New England in 1996, 35-21, and over Pittsburgh in 2010, 31-25). (https://www.packers.com/history/championship-seasons)

Every parent should want their baby to be a champion in life and having them start their existence with a Packer name could be the first step.

Hall of Famers

Over the 100 year history of the NFL 27 players have entered the Pro Football Hall of Fame as Green Bay Packers. Players like Don Hutson, Bart Starr, Brett Favre and Reggie White have come to define what it means to play for the Packers. According to C. David Baker, the President of the Pro Football hall of fame. "A Hall of Famer is someone who has given all they had on and off the field, had a high peak in their career, and was elite at his position."

All parents should want a Hall of Famer child, a person who will grow up to give all to something they are passionate about.

Loyalty to their team

No group of fans is as loyal to their team as the Cheese heads that fill Lambeau Field for everything from practices to playoff games. The Frozen Tundra has been sold out for every game since 1960. According to the Green Bay ticket office, the season-ticket waiting list now has 86,000 names on it, and management estimates a turnover of 90 tickets each year. If you put your name on the list now, you can expect to be attending home games in the year 2067. Despite the nearly 1,000-year waiting list, new names are added to it every season. Every baby deserves to have people around them who are loving and loyal fans of theirs; this could be part of your baby's future if you pick an amazing Packer baby name.

Being a Class Act:

For the Green Bay Packers, winning football games the "right way" has always been important. The organization has always maintained a standard for class and dignity that applies to management, coaches, players and everyone else involved with the franchise. The Packer has long been a reflection of the friendly, blue-collar people that populate Wisconsin.

A winning tradition was established early on in Green Bay, and this has molded the franchise into what it is today. The people involved with the organization have changed, but certain standards have remained. Everyone involved with the franchise is expected to maintain a certain level of esteem for their teammates and the organization. Things in Green Bay are always done in a way that shows respect for the game, the team and the history of the two.

Every Parent wants a baby whose actions they can be proud of, a baby that will grow up to do things the right way.

It should be every parents dream to have a son or daughter that is a Champion in life with a Hall of fame resume that is loyal and a class act. So have fun with this book and good luck finding an amazing baby name for your little cheese head.

Names from the early years of the packers (1919-1956)

In 1919 Curly Lambeau and George Calhoun organized a group of men in Green Bay, Wisconsin into a football team that soon became the best team in the Midwest. Lambeau, a former high school football star, who went on to play college ball at Notre Dame was currently a shipping clerk for the Indian Packing Company when he convinced his employer to donate money for the uniforms and, in the process, lent the nickname "Packers" to the team. With Lambeau serving as head coach and playing halfback, in 1921 the Packers entered the recently formed American Professional Football Association, which a year later would become the NFL.

In the early years the Packers struggled with financial problems to the point of having to forfeit an entire season in 1922. The following year the team became a publicly owned nonprofit corporation supported by the people of Wisconsin and has remained so ever since.

Despite their rough financial start, the Packers won three consecutive championships from 1929 to 1931, with lineups that were laden with future Hall of Famers, including tackle Cal Hubbard, guard Mike Michalske, and halfback John ("Blood") McNally. In 1935 the team added Don Hutson, who proceeded to redefine the wide receiver position and helped the Packers win championships in 1936, 1939, and 1944. Lambeau—who stopped playing for the team in 1929—stepped away from head coaching duties in 1949, and the team struggled for wins throughout the next decade: the Packers posted a losing record seven times between 1950 and 1958. The early years in the Packers history have some legendary names for your baby, however be sure to check out the names to avoid because there are some dozes.

Best baby names from the Early years:

Canadeo - is the last name of Legendary Packer running back Tony Canadeo. Canadeo was the most talented halfback for the

Packers from 1941-1952. In 1949 Tony became the third player in NFL history to rush for 1,000 or more yards in a season. He retired as the Packers' all-time rushing yards leader. Canadeo's jersey number "3" was retired by the Packers immediately following his retirement as a player. He was inducted into the Pro Football Hall of Fame and Wisconsin Athletic Hall of Fame and the Green Bay Packers Hall of Fame.

Canadeo would be a great baby boy name. A baby named after Tony Canadeo could grow up to be an impressive runner with hall of fame talent.

Carmichael – is the last name of Al Carmichael who was a half back and kick returner for the Packers from 1953 to 1958. According to Lee Remmel. Packer historian, Carmichael was known as one of the fastest players during the 1950's and once had 106 yard kick return. Which is still in the record books as the third longest in NFL history.

Carmichael would be an amazing baby boy name. If you name your baby after Al Carmichael he could be super-fast, record setting infant.

Clarke - is the first name of Clark Hinkle. The Packer hall of fame claims Hinkle was widely regarded by teammates and opponents alike as one of the toughest, most talented and dedicated players of the Iron Man Era, which covered the first three decades of pro football. Clark Hinkle played running back for the packers from 1932 to 1941 and was inducted into the pro football hall of fame in 1964.

Clark could be either a boy or Girls name and Hinkle would make for a great middle name. If you name your baby after this Packer legend they could grow up being tough as nails and well respected by their tot peers.

Hutson – is the last name of one of the all-time nfl and packer great Don Hutson. Don Hutson played for the packers from 1935-1945 and was a receiver who redefined the position, he is credited with creating many of the modern pass routes used in the NFL to. Hutson held almost all major receiving records at the time of his retirement, including career receptions, yards, and touchdowns. Even some 75 years later he still holds over 10 NFL records. Don Hutson was a three time nfl Champion, a two time NFL MVP, member of the NFL 75th anniversary team and both a member of the NFL and Green Bay Packers hall of fame.

Hudson would be a lofty name for a baby boy. If you decide to name your baby after Don Hutson he could be an All –Time great record setting person.

Isbell – is the last name of Cecil Isbell, who was a star half back for the Packers from 1938 to 1942. Isbell was one of the best players during the late 1930s being named an All Pro three times. He was also elected to the Packers hall of fame in 1972

Isbell would be a grand name for a baby girl. If you decide to name your baby after Cecil Isbell she could have an super star life.

Kiesling – is the last name of Walt Kiesling, who was one of the best players in the 1920's. Kiesling played only two years for the Packers in 1935 and 1936 but had a big impact on the team's training since he was known for being in tip top shape year round. After his playing career Walt coached for 25 years.

Kiesling would be a good name for both a baby boy and girl. A baby named after Kiesling could be in excellent shape and become a great coach for eternity.

Lambeau – is the Last name of Earl Curly Lambeau. Just in case you are a Packer fan who lives under a rock here is who Curly Lambeau is: According to the Packer hall of fame "Lambeau was the guiding force behind the creation and improbable survival of the small-town Packers in big league football. He also was the team's first star and one of the most successful coaches in NFL history." Not only did Lambeau co-found the packers he also won 6 NFL Championships. Plus not to mention the Packers stadium is named after him.

Lambeau would be an impressive name for a boy or a girl. If you name your baby after curly Lambeau they could be iconic and someone that could be the creator of something special

Lavvie – is the nickname to LaVern "Lavvie" Dilweg who played End for The Packers from 1927 to 1934. He was a three time nfl champion and a member of the 1920s nfl All – Decade team. Dilweg is also in the Green Bay Packer Hall of fame and later in life even represented Wisconsin in the U.S house of Representatives.

Lavvie would be a awesome baby girl's name. A baby named after Lavvie Dilweg could grow up to be a great champion and may even have a career in politics.

Laws – is the last name of Joe Laws, who played halfback and defensive back for the Packers from 1934 to 1945. Law holds the record for intercepting 3 passes in a title game and was known for being one of the best pass defenders of the 1940's.

Laws would be a great baby boy's name. This little bundle of joy could be an interception machine and maybe even become a judge or police officer. Plus as bonus when you put your little bundle of joy down for a nap you can say "I need to lay down the law".

Lewellen – is the last name of Verne Lewellen, who was a back and punter for the packers from 1924-1932. The Packers hall of fame has him down as one of the greatest all-around backs in the NFL's first three decades, Lewellen also was widely regarded as one of the NFL's greatest punters. He was a 3 time all pro player and is also a Packer hall of Famer.

Lewellen would be noble for a baby girl. She could grow up to be a great all-around athlete and person.

McNally – is the last name of john "Blood" McNally one of the most iconic and talented player to ever put on a packer uniform. He played running back from 1929 to 1936. According to the Packer Hall of fame he was born John Victor McNally but adopted the alias Johnny Blood while playing sandlot football and turned it into one of the most magical names in sports. It also was a fitting name for one of the game's most colorful and eccentric players. Most important, Blood was pro football's first big playmaker. McNally played on their first four NFL championship teams and was known for his ability to score from anywhere on the field at any time. He was elected into the NFL hall of fame is 1963.

McNally could be a great name for a boy or a girl. A baby with this name could grow up to be an eccentric legend who's name will echo throughout history.

Remmel - is the last name of Lee Remmel who was a green bay sports writer and then later Green Bay Packers public relations director and team historian. Remmel was an eyewitness to Packers history like few others. He spent nearly three decades writing about them for the Green Bay Press-Gazette. He then spent more than three decades working for the team in public relations and as team historian. As a sportswriter, Remmel chronicled every coach from Curly Lambeau to Dan Devine

Remmel would be a noble name for a baby boy. A baby named after Lee Remmel could grow up with a great appretation for journalism and a love for history.

Rose - is the last name of Al Rose. Al was an end for the Packers from 1932 to 1936. He was best known for being a college star from the University of Texas and for having some of the best hands in the NFL.

Rose is a great name for a baby girl. However instead of telling people your daughter is named after a wussy flower, you can say she was named after Al Rose who was a rough and tumble Packer player.

Tobin – is the first name of Tobin Rote. He played Quart back for the Packers from 1950 to 1956. He was a shining star on some of the Packers worse teams in the history of the organization. Tobin lead the NFL in touch downs twice and was one of the best rushing quarterbacks in history, currently ranked 7th all time.

Tobin would be a nice baby name for a boy. A baby named after Tobin Rote could be a bright spot when everything else around them is dark.

Baby names to avoid:

Boob – is the nickname of "Boob" Bernard Darling, who played center for the Packers from 1927 to 1931. Boob was born and raised in Wisconsin and went to college at Ripon and Beloit Colleges before signing with the Packers. Darling was a great athlete and also played professional basketball for the Oshkosh All-Stars.

Boob is a horrible name for a baby for obvious reasons. In fact Mr. Darling first name Bernard isn't much better for a baby name either.

Buckets – is the nickname of Charles "Buckets" Goldenberg. Buckets was a hall of fame caliber guard for the Packers from 1933 to 1945. He is a member of the 1930s all decade team and went to college at the University of Wisconsin- Madison.

Buckets isn't a good nickname, first name, last name or baby name. Unless your baby is a star basketball player stay away from this name.

Buford - is the first name of Buford "baby" ray. Buford played tackle for the Packers from 1938 to 1948. He is a member of the 1940s all decade team and 4 time all pro.

Buford is an awesome baby name if you want your new family addition to be an offensive lineman. If your baby isn't going to grow up to be 6"6" and 300 plus pounds then maybe choice a different name.

Jug – is the nickname of Francis "Jug" Earp. Jug played center for the Packers from 1922 to 1932. His claim to fame is being one of the first pro football players to snap the ball with one hand. Jug Earp is a Packer hall of famer who was elected in 1970.

No parents want to say here is my baby Jug. Honestly, Mr. Earp's real name Francis probably should be avoided as well unless he is a talking horse (joke for the grandparents).

Michalske - is the last name of NFL great Mike Michalske. According to the Packer Hall of Fame Michalske is "Widely regarded as one of the greatest guards in the first 30 years of the NFL." Michalske was a member of the 1920's All-Decade team and was elected into the Pro football hall of fame in 1964.

Michalske was an amazing player but a lozey baby name. the name is just hard to pronounce and doesn't role off the tongue well.

Milt – is the first name of Milt Gantenbein. Milt played ten years with the Packers from 1931 to 1940. He was a member of 3 world championship teams and grew up in Lacrosse, Wisconsin.

Milt was a great name in the 1930's however in 2019 the name is rarely ever heard. So parents I encourage you to keep this name in the past.

Tiny - is the nickname of Paul "tiny" Engebretsen. Tiny was an offensive lineman for the pack from 1934 to 1941. He Was a member of 3 NFL championship teams. In 1978, Engebretsen was elected into the Packers hall of fame.

Tiny is a good ironic nickname but as a baby name not so much. Maybe go with Mr. Engebretsen given name of Paul if you like classics.

Tubby - is the nickname of Lynn Tubby Howard. Tubby played for the Packers from 1921 to 1922. He is a Native son to Wisconsin and was born and raised in the small town of Mondovi.

Tubby is a baby name to stay far away from. Though there has been a few successful Tubby's in this world such as Basketball coach Tubby smith, there is more of a chance you will give your new bundle of joy a life-long complex.

Wildung- is the last name of Dick Wildung. Dick played tackle for the Packers from 1946 to 1953. He is a member of both the college football hall of fame and the Green Bay Packers hall of fame.

Wildung just doesn't have a good ring to it and any name with the word dung in it may not be the first choice.

Zatkoff – is the last name of Roger Zatkoff. Roger played for the packers from 1953 to 1956. During that time he was a standout linebacker who went to the Pro Bowl in 1954, 1955, 1956. The University of Michigan give an Award to the team's best Linebacker each year named after Zatkoff.

Zatkoff was a legendary college player and a stand out packer however this name just doesn't sound good as a baby name.

Names from the Lombardi era

The team's most successful period was in the 1960s, under the legendary coach Vince Lombardi, who had been hired in 1959. Lombardi's Packer teams in the '60s were stocked with talent, boasting future Hall of Fame players on offense and defense: quarterback Bart Starr, fullback Jim Taylor, halfback Paul Hornung, tackle Forrest Gregg, linebacker Ray Nitschke, end Willie Davis, tackle Henry Jordan, cornerback Herb Adderley, and safety Willie Wood. They won championships in 1961 and 1962 and followed with three straight championships starting in the 1965–66 season. On January 15, 1967, in the inaugural Super Bowl, the Packers defeated the Kansas City Chiefs 35–10. They successfully defended their Super Bowl title the following year against the Oakland Raiders, 33–14. The Lombardi era is loaded with amazing football players who have impressive names that live on in history. This is a great era to find a baby name!!

Best Baby names in the Lombardi era

Adderley - is the last name of Herb Adderley. Herb was an all-decade cornerback who played on 6 national championship teams. Herb Adderley was also a great return guy on special teams and was known for his lightning fast speed.

Adderley would be a awesome name for a baby girl. A baby girl named after this Hall of Fame great could grow up to be a true champion and be very swift.

Aldridge - is the last name of Lionel Aldridge. Lionel was a defensive end for the Packers from 1963 to 1971. He was a three time NFL Champion and a member of the Green Bay Packers Hall of Fame.

Aldridge would be a nice name for a baby boy. A baby named after this tough as nails defensive player could grow up sacking quarterbacks and making goal line stands in championship games.

Bart – is the first name of all-time great Green bay packer, Bart Starr. Starr is one of only 6 Packers in the last 100 years to have his number retired. Bart Starr also was the field general for 5 NFL championship teams. This man is an iconic Packer and should be one of the first names that comes up when naming your new baby.

Bart would be an amazing name for a baby boy. A baby named after Bart Starr could grow up to an all-time great person.

Bobby Dillon – is the full name of one of the greatest and under-rated Packer players of all time. Dillion is the Packers all-time leader in interceptions and was a 4 time all pro player. He did all of this with just one working eye.

Bobby Dillon could be a great name for a baby boy. A baby named Bobby Dillion could grow up to be an interception machine. The best part is if you ever stop liking the Packers you can shorten your babies name to Bob Dillion and say he was named after the legendary folk singer.

Boyd – is the first name of Boyd Dowler. He was an all-star wide receiver and punter from 1959 to 1969. Boyd was named rookie of the year in 1959. He also was a member of the 1960s all decade team and was a 5 time NFL champion.

Boyd would be a good baby boy's name. A baby named after Boyd Dowler could grow up with amazing hands and a strong kicking leg.

Chandler – is the last name of Don Chandler. Chandler was the Packers kicker and punter from 1965 to 1967. He was one of the best kickers of the 1960s and was named to the all-decade team. Don Chandler was also voted into the Packers hall of fame in 1975.

Chandler would be a wonderful name for both a baby girl and a baby boy. A baby named after Chandler could be a great kicker with a champion leg. Chandler is also a good compromise name for you and your wife. She could tell people your baby is named after some wussy TV character and you can tell your friends the truth he was named after a legendary kicker.

Currie – is the last name of Dan Currie, who was a linebacker for the Packers from 1958 to 1964. Dan is a two time world champion and was known as one of the hardest hitting defensive players in the 1960s era.

Currie would be a great name for a baby girl. A baby named after Dan Currie could grow up to be a dependable defense player and a true champion.

Forrest – is the First name of Legendary tackle Forrest Gregg. Gregg was a key player on the Packers dynasty of head coach Vince Lombardi that won five NFL championships and the first two Super Bowls in the 1960s. He played mostly at right tackle, but also filled in at guard. Gregg earned an "iron-man" tag by playing in a then-league record 188 consecutive games in sixteen seasons, from 1956 until 1971.

Forrest would be a great baby boy name. If your new baby is named Forrest he could grow up to be a great blocker who will be trustworthy to not miss a game.

Hanner - is the last name of Dave Hanner. This gentleman, dedicated 42 years of his life to the Green Bay Packers. Hanner played defense tackle from 1952 to 1964. After the 1964 season he became a coach and then later on a scout for the Packers. Very few men have been as loyal to the Packers as Dave. Hanner.

Hanner would be a good name for a baby boy. If you name your new baby after Dave Hanner he could be one of the devoted packer fans ever. Just be sure to stay away from Hanner's nick name when naming your baby. He was commonly known as "Hawg" Hanner.

Gillingham - is the last name of Gale Gillingham, who played for the Packers from 1966 to 1976. During his playing time Gillingham was named all-pro 6 times and was a member of two nfl championship teams. Gale Gillingham was one of the strongest Packers ever and was known for spending hours in the weight room which helped contribute to his ten years of dominance.

Gillingham would be a amazing name for a baby boy. A baby named after this packer great could grow up to be a powerful blocker and a world champion.

Jeter - is the last name of Bob Jeter. Jeter was a hard hitting corner back who was part of three of Lombardi's Championship teams. He was also a two time pro bowler and is in the Green Bay Packers hall of fame.

Jeter would be a great baby name for either a girl or a boy. A baby named after Bob Jeter could grow up to be a great pass defender or maybe a shortstop for the Yankee.

Jordan – is the last name of hall of famer Henry Jordan. Jordan was a stout defensive tackle for ten years. During this time Henry Jordan was a 7 times all-pro and 5 time world champion.

Jordan would be a great name for a baby girl or boy. A baby named after Henry Jordan could grow up to be an amazing defensive player or maybe even a basketball player.

Kramer – is the last name of Jerry Kramer, who played from 1958 to 1968 for the Green Bay Packers. Kramer is one of the most popular Packer players of all-time. He was a 5 time nfl Champion and a member of the 1960s all-decade team. Jerry Kramer is also known for his best-selling book called "Instant Replay" and finally was voted into the Pro Football hall of fame in 2018.

Kramer would be a great name for either a boy or a girl. A baby named after Kramer could grow up to be a great ambassador for the Green Bay Packers and maybe even an amazing author as well.

Max McGee - is the full name of the Lombardi eras best wide receiver. He is a five time NFL champion and a member of the Green Bay Packers hall of fame. Max McGee is also famous for being a celebrity restaurateur, having co-founded the restaurant Chi-Chi's.

Max McGee is a nice name for a baby boy. A baby named after Max McGee could grow up with great hands and may even open a bunch of steak houses and southwest Mex restaurants.

Mercein – is the last name of Chuck Mercein. Chuck played for the Packers from 1967-to 1969. Mercein was born and raised in the Milwaukee, Wisconsin area. He was also well known for his brain as well as his brawn as he graduated college from Yale.

Mercein would be a noble name for a baby girl. A baby named after Chick Mercein could grow up having big muscles and a even bigger brain.

Nitschke - is the last name of all-time great Packer Ray Nitschke. Ray was one of the greatest linebackers in NFL history and was known for his toughness. Nitschke is one of only 6 players in Packer history to have his number retired.

Nitschke is not a name for just any baby. A baby named after Ray Nitschke will grow up being one bad ass S.O.B. and as parents you better be ready.

Ringo – is the Last name of Jim Ringo, who played center for the Packers from 1953 to 1963. Ringo was a 10 time Pro Bowl center and two time NFL championship. Jim Ringo was a member of the 1960's All Decade team and was voted into the Pro football hall of fame in 1981.

Ringo is a great baby name for a baby boy. A baby named after this Packer Hall of famer could be an all-time great at snapping the football.

Starr - is the last name of Bart Starr. Yes, His first name was already mentioned but this man is so nice his name is on the list twice.

Starr would be an absolute amazing name for a baby girl. A Baby girl named after Bart Starr would truly shine in life.

Taylor – is the last name of packer great Jim Taylor. Mr. Taylor was a hard running fullback from 1958 to 1966. During his time in Green bay he was named NFL mvp in 1962 and was a member of 4 championship teams. According to most defensive players from the 1960s Jim Taylor was the hardest man in football to tackle.

Taylor would be a great baby name for either a boy or a girl. A baby named after this impressive hall of famer could grow up to be tough as nails and not easy to tackle. Remember to remind people your baby is NOT named after an annoying blonde pop singer.

Thurston – is the last name of Fred "Fuzzy" Thurston. Fuzzy was a member of the legendary Packers offensive line from the 1960's. Thurston is a home grown Wisconsin guy, growing up in Altoona and is one of only a handful of NFL players who was a member of 6 championship teams.

Thurston is a hall of fame baby name for a boy. A baby name after Fuzzy Thurston could grow up to lead the famous packer sweep or maybe open up some restaurants.

Vince - is the first name of Vince Lombardi. Lombardi is the Greatest coach in NFL history, Period. No coach in National Football League history achieved more success in less time than Lombardi did during his nine seasons in Green Bay. He won five NFL championships, including Super Bowls I and II, and compiled a remarkable 89-29-4 regular-season record. Lombardi was also one of the greatest leaders in the history of America.

Vince is an all-time great green bay packer's baby name. The only reason you do not name your baby Vince is because you already have three kids named Vince and your house is getting kind of confusing with so many Vince's running around.

Baby names to avoid

Cochran – is the last name of long time Packers coach and scout John "Red" Cochran. Cochran worked for the Packers for 42 years which is one of the longest tenures of anyone in football operations over the storied life of the franchise.

Red was a great coach and football man however a baby named Cochran just sound wrong for so many reasons. No parent should be at a park yell "Cochran, come here"!

Fleming – is the last name of Marv Fleming, a tight end for the Packers from 1963 to 1969. Fleming was part of 5 nfl championship teams during his career and is a member of the Green Bay Packer hall of fame.

Marv is a true champion on and off the field, however no parent wants a baby that could also be named after thick, stringy mucus created in the respiratory tract as a result of pathogens.

Hathcock – is the last name of Dave Hathcock. Dave only played one season for the packer but that season was the year the Packers won super bowl 1.

Hathcock is a name you want to stay away from for your little bundle of joy. After all no one wants to go to the park and have to ask other parents if they have seen your little Hathcock.

Hornung - is the last name of Green Bay Packers "golden boy", Paul Hornung. Paul was one of the greatest running backs of all time, having won the Heisman trophy in college for being the best college player which was followed up by an mvp in 1961 while playing on one of the greatest Packer teams of all time.

Hornung was one of the most impressive players to ever put on the green and gold, however a baby name after this legend is not a good idea do to the fact his name sounds so much like horny.

Kostelnik - is the last name of Ron Kostelnik, who played for the packers from 1961 to 1968. Ron was a 5 time nfl champion and is a member of the Green bay Packer hall of fame.

Kostelnik had a steady nfl career, however this name just doesn't roll of the tongue and because of that you should maybe just name your baby Ron.

Zeke - is the first name of Zeke Bratkowski, who was the backup quarterback in Green Bay from 1963 to 1968. Bratkowski later became a coach for the Packers and is a member of the National Polish sports Hall of fame.

Zeke was a loyal Packer Backer for many years however his name just doesn't seem to fit with modern baby names and should be avoided.

Names from the dark ages aka 1970's and 80s

For about a quarter-century after Lombardi's departure, the Packers had relatively little on-field success. In the 22 seasons from 1968 to 1989, they had only five seasons with a winning record, one being the shortened 1982 strike season. They appeared in the playoffs twice, with a 1–2 record. The period saw five different head coaches – Phil Bengtson, Dan Devine, Bart Starr, Forrest Gregg, and Lindy Infante – two of whom, Starr and Gregg, were Lombardi's era stars, while Bengtson was a former Packer coach. Each led the Packers to a worse record than his predecessor. Poor personnel decisions were rife, notoriously the 1974 trade by acting general manager Dan Devine which sent five 1975 or 1976 draft picks (two first-rounders, two second-rounders and a third) to the Los Angeles Rams for aging quarterback John Hadl, who would spend only 1½ seasons in Green Bay.[19] Another came in the 1989 NFL Draft, when offensive lineman Tony Mandarich was taken with the second overall pick ahead of Barry Sanders, Deion Sanders, and Derrick Thomas. Though rated highly by nearly every professional scout at the time, Mandarich's performance failed to meet expectations, earning him ESPN's ranking as the third "biggest sports flop" in the last 25 years.

Though the teams during this era of Packer history sucked there were some outstanding names to choose from for your bundle of joy. Here is a comprehensive list to choose from:

The best names from the 1970s and 1980s

Brockington – is the last name of John Brockington. John was a star running back for the Packers in the 1970s. He was named to 3 pro bowls and was the rookie of the year in 1971. John Brockington was known for his strength and powerful running style which would punish anyone who tried to tackle him.

Brockington would be a great baby boy's name. A baby boy named after John Brockington could grow up to be very formidable athlete who know one with a "right mind" would want to mess with.

Buchanon – is the last name of Willie Buchanon, who was a cornerback for the Packers from 1972 to 1978. During his Packer career he was a two time pro bowl player and was the defense rookie of the year.

Buchanon would be an awesome name for a baby boy. A baby named after Willie Buchanon could end up growing up with great cover skills and may even set a record for having 4 interceptions in one game.

Carr- is the last name of Green Bay Packer linebacker Fred Carr. Fred was one of the best defensive players in the 1970s. In fact he was a 3 time pro bowler and a Green Bay Packer hall of famer.

Carr would be a great baby girl or boy name. A baby named after Fred Carr could grow up to be a dominate defensive force to be reckoned with.

Coffman – is the last name of one of Green Bay's greatest tight end, Paul Coffman. Paul is a member of the Green Bay Packers hall of fame and was known of having the best combination of catching and blocking ability in the nfl during the 1980s.

Coffman would be a wonderful name for a baby boy. A baby names after Paul Coffman could grow up to be a pro bowl person with an amazing head of curly hair.

Devine- is the last name of former Packers Coach Dan Devine. Dan was the Green Bay Packers head coach and general manager from 1971 to 1974. He was also a very successful college coach and was elected into the college football hall of fame.

Devine would be a decent name for a baby girl. A baby named after Dan Devine could grow up to become a great leader.

However she may also give up a bunch of draft picks for a "has-been" quarterback.

Ellis- is the last name of Green Bay Packer Gerry Ellis. Gerry was a hardtop tackle running back for the pack from 1980 to 1986. Ellis is also a member of the Green Bay Packers hall of fame.

Ellis would be a nice baby name for a little boy. A baby named after Gerry Ellis could grow up being fast and strong with great hands out of the backfield.

Harris- is the last name of Green Bay Packers defensive stud Tim Harris. Harris was a Packer linebacker from 1986- to 1990, he was a two time pro-bowler and in 1989 was defensive player of the year having recorded 19.5 sacks.

Harris would be a great baby name for either a baby boy or girl. A baby named after Tim Harris could grow up to be a sack machine who love to break out the "six shooters".

John Jefferson – is the full name of one of Green Bay's most dynamic wide receivers in the 1980s. John was a four time pro bowler and a member of a number of different football hall of fames.

John Jefferson would be a amazing name for a baby boy. A baby named after this Packer great could grow up to league the NFL in receiving yards and may have a buddy named James Lofton that he will be partners in crime with

MacArthur – is the first name of MacArthur Lane, who played for the Packers from 1972 to 1974. Lane was a scoring machine and once scored 11 touchdowns in one season. He was also known for his powerful running and was nicknamed the truck.

MacArthur would be a good name for a baby boy. A Baby named after MacArthur lane could grow up to be someone that is hard to bring down and has the impact power of an automobile.

McCarren - is the last name of Packer Great and long-time radio announcer Larry McCarren. Larry was a pro bowl center who was known as the "rock" for his ability to play in 162 consecutive games.

McCarren would be a amazing name for a baby boy. A baby named after Larry McCarren could grow up to be great at snapping the football and an amazing play-by-play commentator.

Lofton - is the last name of James Lofton. James played wide receiver for the Packers from 1978 to 1986 and was an 8 time pro bowler. Lofton was one of the only players to catch a touchdown pass in the 1970s, 1980s, 1990's and is a member of both the Green Bay Packers and Pro football hall of fame.

Lofton would be a great name for a baby boy or girl. A baby named after this Packer great could grow up to be an all decade person and may be seen hanging out with babies named Lynn dickey and John Jefferson.

Odom - is the last name of Steve Odom, who was a wide receiver and kick returner for the Packers from 1974 to 1979. Odom was one of the best punt returners in the game and holds the Packers record for returning a punt 95 yards for a touchdown against the bears in 1974.

Odom would be a nice name for a baby boy. A baby named after Steve Odom could grow up to have tremendous speed to go along with hands that can catch everything thrown his way.

Stenerud - is the last name of Packers kicker Jan Stenerud. Jan is a hall of fame kicker who played for the Packers from 1980 to 1983. He was also named to the NFL 75th anniversary team.

Jan Stenerud is one of the greatest special team's players in the history of the NFL.

Stenerud would be a great name for a baby boy. A baby name named after Jan Stenerud could grow up to have an amazing kicking leg and could be known as one of the greatest.

Baby names to avoid:

Dickey - is the last name of the beloved Packer quarterback Lynn Dickey. Lynn is a Packer Hall of Famer and was one of the Best passers in the 1980s. However, no one wants to have to ask the neighbors if they saw their "little Dickey".

Dilweg – is the last name of former Packer Quarterback Anthony Dilweg. Anthony was a good college quarterback and was a back-up in Green Bay for 3 year. Though Anthony Dilweg is a nice guy is last name should be avoided for your new baby.

John Hadl - is a the full name of the quarterback who the Packers traded for in one of the worse deals in Football history. The Packers traded five draft picks—first and second round picks for 1975 and 1976, as well as a third round pick in 1975. (yes this was mentioned like 5 times) Hadle ended up not doing anything as a starter in Green Bay. This name is to be avoided not because John Hadle was a bad player or a bad person but because the pain that most packer fans feel when thinking about the trade he was associated with.

Majkowski - is the last name of Don Majkowski. Don was a Packer from 1987 to 1992 and was a pro-bowler and passing leader during that time. Majkowski was the quarterback who got injured and started the Brett Favre era.

Majkowski is a name that just does not roll of the tongue well and should be avoided unless you live in Pulaski, or Stevens Point Wisconsin where a large amount of Polish people live. In these communities the name Majkowski is very common and in most classrooms there will be two or three little Majkowski running around. On a personal note I think my cousin in Stevens Point named there new son Majkowski Kuskeski.

Mandarich – is the last name of Packers first round draft pick bust Tony Mandarich. Referred to as "the best offensive line prospect ever",[Mandarich was highly touted during his collegiate career at Michigan State, leading to his high selection in the 1989 draft by the Packers. However, Mandarich was unable to live up to expectations and was released following four seasons with the team

Mandarich is a named to avoid since he is one of the most disliked person in Packer history. He is disliked not only because he did not live up to expectations but because he was a jerk of a person to many in the community.

Sweeny – is the nick name of Clarence "Sweeny" Williams. Sweeny was a Packer from 1970 to 1977 and was a solid Defense End during his career. However a baby named Sweeny might not be able to have the same respect throughout life as a 6'5" 265lb football would. So I advise avoiding this Packer player name for your baby's sake.

Woodfield - is the last name of Randall Woodfield. He was a wide receiver drafted in the 17th round in 1974. ***All you have to do is google the name Randall Woodfield and you will know why no baby EVER should have this name. ***

Brett Favre era names

In 1992 the Packers traded for a little known quarterback named Brett Favre, who would become the key piece in the team's renaissance in the 1990s up until the mid-2000. Beginning in 1993, Green Bay qualified for the postseason in six straight years, including two NFC championships and subsequent trips to the Super Bowl. The team's third Super Bowl appearance, in 1997, was a success: they defeated the New England Patriots 35–21. However, they did not repeat their win the following year against the Denver Broncos. During this tine Brett Favre was the best player in the NFL becoming the only player to win three straight MVP awards but the team remained a play-off contender into the 21st century. Favre acrimoniously left the Packers in 2008, and the Packers' offense was given over to young star quarterback Aaron Rodgers.

The Favre era has some of the best baby names in all of Packer history. Look though the following list a pick a good one!

The top baby names from the Favre era.

Barnett – is the last name of long time Packer linebacker Nick Barnett. Nick was a first round pick in 2003 and was both a Super Bowl Champion and all pro during his Packer career.

Barnett would be a good name for a baby boy. A baby named after Nick Barnett could grow up to be a great tackler with amazing sideline to sideline speed.

Bennett - is the last name of Edgar Bennett. Edgar was one of the premier running backs for the Packers in the 1990s. In fact he was the first Packer to rush for 1,000 yards in a generation. Edgar Bennett was part of the great super bowl 31 team and is a member of the Green Bay Packers Hall of Fame.

Bennett is a great name for a baby boy. A baby named after Edgar Bennett could grow up to be a dependable runner who is a good football player and great person.

Brett Favre – is the full name of one Packers all-time greats. Favre was one of the people responsible for turning around the Packer organization from 20 plush years of being a laughing stock of the NFL.

Brett holds many NFL records, including most career pass attempts and most consecutive starts by a player. At the time of his retirement, he was the NFL's all-time leader in passing yards, passing touchdowns and quarterback wins; all three records have since been broken.

Brett Favre would be a amazingt name for a baby boy. A baby named after this legend could grow up to be an exciting to watch gun slinging all-time great.

Brooks - is the last name of Robert Brooks. Robert Brooks was one of the star receivers of the 1990's for the Packers. Brooks is known for two major events, one being having the longest touchdown in Packers history, the second is making the Lambeau leap (which Leroy butler invented) popular with his rap song "Jump in the Stands".

Brooks would be a nice name for a baby girl or boy. A baby named after Robert Brooks could grow up to have great speed and amazing hands to go along with a smile that could light up a room.

Bubba - is the nick name of tight end, Daniel BUBBA Franks. Bubba was a 3 time pro bowler and was one of Brett Favre's favorite red zone targets in the early 2000s.

Bubba would be an amazing name for a baby boy. A baby named after Bubba could grow up to be an all-American giant target in the back of the end zone.

Butler - is the last name of Leroy Butler. Leroy was one of the best Safeties during the 1990s. He was a four time all-pro player and the first player in NFL history to record 20 sacks and 20 interceptions. Butler was also the first Packer to Jump in the stands after Reggie White recovered a fumble and flipped it to him where he went into the end zone.

Butler would be a awesome name for a baby boy. A baby named after Leroy Butler could grow up to be a hall of fame defender or maybe answering the door for Bruce Wayne.

Clifton – is the last name of long time offensive tackle, Chad Clifton. Chad established a reputation as one of the NFL's best and unheralded blindside blockers for Brett Favre. He Was a two time pro-bowler and a Packer hall of famer.

Clifton would be a nice name for a baby boy. A baby named after Chad Clifton could grow up to be a super bowl champion who would be impossible to "get the corner on"

Desmond – is the first name of Packer special teams star Desmond Howard. Desmond was a college superstar winning the Heisman trophy before coming to the Packers. While on the Packers he was the super bowl 31 mvp and an all-pro player.

Desmond would be an awesome name for a baby boy. A baby named after Desmond Howard could grow up to have a 90 yard punt return for a touchdown in the Super bowl and rack up a ton of all-purpose yards during their career.

Detmer - is the last name of quarterback Ty Detmer. Ty was Brett Favre's back up from 1992-1995. He is most famous for winning the Heisman trophy in 1990.

Detmer would be an nice name for a baby boy. A baby named after Ty Detmer could grow up to a an All American college football player and an overall nice guy.

Dorsey - is the first name of Packers running back, Dorsey Levens. Dorsey was a great combination of a power rusher along with a great pair of receiving hands. He was a pro bowler in 1997 and is also a member of the Green Bay Packer hall of fame.

Dorsey would be a fine name for a baby boy. A baby named after Dorsey Levens could grow up to run like a horsy.

Favre - is the last name of all-time great Brett Favre. His name is on this list twice because he was such a great Packer and because there are a ton (like five) of grade school kids running around Wisconsin with this name. Remember that though Brett is a boy's name. his last name would be great for a baby boy or girl or anything that needs a name.

Ferguson – is the last name of wide receiver, Robert Ferguson. Robert was a second round pick of the Packers in 2001 and was one of Brett Favre's favorite targets for five years.

Ferguson would be a nice name for a baby boy. A baby named after Robert Ferguson could grow up to have dependable hands and the ability to make amazing catches in big games.

Harlan - is the last name of former Green Bay Packers president, Bob Harlan. During Harlan's 19 years as head of the organization, the Packers won a Super Bowl and became one of the NFL's exemplary franchises. He also put the franchise on firm financial footing for years to come as the driving force behind the redevelopment of Lambeau Field as a year-round destination.

Harlan would make a great name for a baby boy or girl. A baby named after Bob Harlan could grow up to make tough and defining decisions that could turnaround a franchise. More importantly your baby could grow up to be an amazing person with a big heart.

Hawk - is the last name of Packers linebacker, A.J. Hawk. A.J was the Packers first round draft pick in 2006 and was a reliable starter for 8 years. He was a major part of the super bowl XLV and while in college was one of the greatest linebackers to ever play for Ohio State.

Hawk would be a good name for a baby boy. A baby named after A.J Hawk could grow up to be a dependable tackler who wants to have his crib in a hyperbolic chamber.

Holmgren - is the last name of coach Mike Holmgren. According to the Packers hall of fame, Holmgren accomplished what five head coaches before him had failed to do: He returned the Packers to prominence. Not since Vince Lombardi stepped down after winning his third straight NFL championship in 1967 had a Packers coach departed Green Bay with a winning record. But over Holmgren's seven seasons, he led them to their first Super Bowl title in 29 years; compiled a .670 winning percentage in the regular-season, a figure topped only by Lombardi; and finished on the plus side of .500 every year, something the Packers had done only four times over their previous 24 years. (site Packer hall of fame)

Holmgren would be a great name for a baby boy. A baby named after Mike Holmgren could grow up to be a championship coach who would be an composed play caller under pressure and would have an amazing mustache.

Gilbert - is the first name of one of Packers fan favorites, Gilbert Brown. Gilbert was the big man in the middle of the Packers defense who was great at stopping the run. He was known for his big heart and big stomach. In fact he ate so much burger king that they named a burger for him.

Gilbert would be a amazing name for a baby boy. A baby named after Gilbert Brown could grow up to be larger than life and if he doesn't have a career in football he could always be a gravedigger.

Jacke - is the last name of Packers long time kicker, Chris Jacke. Chris was an all-pro in 1993 and a member of the Green Bay Packers hall of fame. He is also one of the top scorers in Packer history.

Jacke would be an nice name for a baby girl. A baby named after Chris Jacke could grow up to kick field goals in the super bowl and could have some amazing "90's" hair.

Jennings - is the last name of Packers wide receiver, Greg Jennings. Greg is a two time pro-bowler and a super bowl champion. He was one of Brett Favre's favorite receivers later in his career.

Jennings would be an fine baby name for a baby boy or girl. A baby named after Greg Jennings could grow up having amazing hands to go with explosive speed. This baby is will be ready to make big plans on and off the football field.

Jervey - is the last name of running back, Travis Jervey. Travis Jervey was the first Packer to make the pro-bowl as a special team player. He was also known for his free spirit and love for surfing which in some cases he may have loved more than football.

Jervey would be a great name for a baby boy or girl. A baby named after Travis Jervey could grow up having amazing combination of speed and strength. They could also have a pet lion named Nala (true story).

Kampman – is the last name of long time defensive end, Aaron Kampman. Aaron was one of the best Packer on the defense side of the ball from 2002 to 2009. During that time Kampman amassed 58 sacks and was a two time pro-bowler.

Kampman would be an amazing name for a baby boy. A baby named after Aaron Kampman could grow up to be relentless when sacking the quarterback or be a nice farm boy from Iowa.

McGarrahan - is the last name of Scott McGarrahan. Scott was a safety for the Green Bay Packers from 1998 to 2000 and contributed to the great super bowl 31 defense.

McGarrahan would be a good name for a baby boy. A baby named after Scott McGarrahan could grow up to be a defense back.

McKenzie - is the last time of Packers long time Corner back, Mike McKenzie. Mike was a third round draft pick by the Packers in 1999 and became the starter in the Defensive backfield for the next ten years.

McKenzie would be a nice name for a baby girl. A baby named after Mike McKenzie could grow up to be a dependable defensive player and super bowl champion.

Na'il – is the first name of Na'il Diggs, who played for the packers from 2000-2005. Diggs was known for his hard hits and ability to get to the quarterback. Na'il was also known for his ability to block kicks on special teams.

Na'il would be an amazing name for a baby boy. A baby named after Na'il Diggs could grow up to be feared by quarterbacks everywhere. Being big, strong and fast would be a great way to grow up.

Navies - is the last name of former packer linebacker, Hannibal Navies. Hannibal was a steady linebacker and special team's player for the pack from 2003 to 2004.

Navies would be an awesome name for a baby boy or girl. A baby named after Hannibal Navies could grow up to be a speedy tackling machine that could both sack and intercept the quarterback.

Paris - is the first name of former Packer Linebacker, Paris Lenon. Paris was a Packer from 2001- 2005 and played a major role both on defense but also on special teams.

Paris would be a great name for a baby girl. A baby named after Paris Lenon could grow up to be a swift, powerful hitting defender or maybe a reality TV star.

Pederson – is the last name of long time back-up quarterback, Doug Pederson. Doug was the back up to the great Brett Favre from 1995-1998 and then again from 2001- 2004. During his time in Green Bay Pederson was also the holder on field goals.

Pederson would be a great name for a baby boy. A baby named after Doug Pederson could grow up to have the best job on the planet. He could also grow up to be a super bowl champion coach.

Reggie - is the first name of Packers legend Reggie White. Reggie was one of the greatest football players ever. During his career he was a two-time NFL Defensive Player of the Year, 13-time Pro Bowl, and 13-time All-Pro selection holds second place all-time among career sack leaders with 198 (behind Bruce Smith's 200 career sacks) and was selected to the NFL 75th Anniversary All-Time Team, NFL 1990s All-Decade Team, and the NFL 1980s All-Decade Team.

Reggie would be an amazing name for a baby boy. A baby named after Reggie White could grow up to be the best defensive player to ever play in the NFL.

Rison – is the last name of Wide Receiver, Andre Rison. Andre had a very brief Green Bay Packer career but will always be remembered for his big catch in Super Bowl 31.

Rison would be a nice baby name for a baby boy or girl. A bay named after Andre Rison could grow up to be an amazing deep threat that may need some TLC.

Rivera - is the last name of Packers all-star guard Marco Rivera. Marco Played for Green Bay from 1996 to 2004. During that time, Marco was a 3 time pro bowler, super bowl champ and in 2011 was voted into the Packers Hall of Fame.

Rivera would be a great name for a baby girl or baby boy. A baby named after Marco Rivera could grow up to be an athletic, all pro offensive lineman who will be a noble person on and off the field.

Samkon - is the first name of former Green Bay Packers running back, Samkon Gado. Though only a packer for a very short time (2005-2006) his name still has a place in the hearts of many fans. Samkon was undrafted out of Liberty college and came to the Packers in a pinch when there were no running backs healthy to play.

Samkon would be an awesome name for a baby boy. A baby named after Samkon could grow up to be a fan favorite player and even more important an ENT physician.

Sterling - is the first name of Packer great Sterling Sharpe. Sterling Sharpe was one of the greatest wide receivers in Packer history and if it wasn't for an injury that cut his career short he would have been one of the NFL's all-time greats. During his short career Sharpe was a 5 time pro bowler and led the league in receptions 3 times.

Sterling would be a nice name for a baby boy or girl. A baby named after Sterling Sharpe could grow up to have an amazing combination of speed and strength that would resulting in catching tons of touchdowns.

Sydney - is the last name of Packers full back and coach Harry Sydney. Harry is a three time super bowl champion and the only person to catch a touch down from all-time greats Brett Favre and Joe Montana.

Sydney would be an amazing baby girl's name. A baby named after Harry Sydney could grow up to be a special team's superstar who has an impact off the field as a mentor and a leader in their community.

Winters - is the last name of Packers long time center, Frank Winters. Frank was a pro bowl player and is in the Green Bay Packer hall of fame. He, along with Brett Favre and Mark Chmura were known as the three Packerinos.

Winters would be a amazing name for a baby girl. A baby named after Frank Winters could grow up to be a dependable snapper with a great love for donuts.

Wolf - is the last name of NFL hall of fame, General Manager, Ron Wolf. Ron Wolf is widely credited with bringing success to a Packers franchise that had rarely won during the two decades prior. Some of Ron Wolf's greatest accomplishments are trading for a young Brett Favre and bring in one of the all-time great free agents to the Packers. During Ron Wolf's career he has been involved in Winning three super bowls.

Wolf would be a great name for a baby boy. A baby named after Ron Wolf could grow up to put together championship teams and be a great leader of men.

Packers Names to Avoid:

Cletidus – is the first name of former Packer defensive lineman, Cletidus Hunt. Besides the fact Cletidus is name that just doesn't roll off the tongue, it also doesn't help that during his short career he signed a huge contract and never came close to living up to it. So Cletidus as a baby name should be avoided.

Galbreath – is the last name of long time offensive lineman Harry Galbreath. Harry was a dependable blocker for almost a decade in the NFL, however a Harry Galbreath sounds like something a doctor should check out not a little bundle of joy.

Gbaja-Biamila - is the last name of one of the Packers all-time great pass rushers, Kabeer Gbaja-Biamila is a Packer hall of famer and all around awesome guy, however this name is just too damn long and hard to say. Parents are very busy taking care of their kids and don't want to have to spend 5 minutes every time they have to write their kids name.

Jamal – is the first name of the Packers first round draft pick Jamal Reynolds. Jamal was supposed to be the next pass rushing, quarterbacking sacking stud for the Packers. However he ended up only getting 3 sacks in 3 seasons and was out of the NFL by 2004. Jamal should be avoided as a baby name since you don't want your baby to be a disappointment that never lives up to expectations.

McMahon – is the last name of one time backup quarterback Jim McMahon. Yes, Jim Mcmahon was a Packer in 1995 and 1996 and even was part of the super bowl 31 team. The reason to avoid this name is not only was he a long time Chicago bears quarterback, the also is kind of a big jerk too.

Najeh – Is the first name of former Packer running back Najeh Davenport. Najeh was a third down back and a great compliment to Ahman Green in the Packers backfield during the early 2000s. The name Najeh should be avoided since it will always be associated with an innocent that occurred when Mr. Davenport was in college that earned him the nickname "dookie" and the "dump truck". A baby should be going in their diapers only!

Tauscher – is the last name of long time Packer offensive lineman, Mark Tauscher. Mark Is a hometown hero who grew up in Auburndale, Wisconsin, played football at UW Madison and then spend 10 years with the Packers. However having a little Tauscher running around invokes a vision of a baby that weighs 400lbs with no muscle mass. Maybe some people wouldn't mind a BIG bundle of joy but personally I want to be able to pick up my baby and hold it when it's sad.

Aaron Rodgers era names

After backing up Brett Favre for the first three years of his NFL career, Rodgers became the Packers' starting quarterback in 2008 and has been one of the NFL's premier quarterbacks for last 12 years. The Highlight of this era has been the victory in Super Bowl XLV over the Pittsburgh Steelers. Also during the Rodgers era the Packers went to the Playoff's nine or the lasr13 years. This era has produced a lot of Winning football and a emenze number of great players with amazing names. If you are looking for a modern name of a Champion take a gander of the list below:

Best names from this era:

Aaron Rodgers – is the first and last name of one of the Packers all–time great quarterbacks. Aaron Rodgers is known by many as the most talented quarterback in the NFL. He is a three time league most valuable player awards and an seven time Pro bowler. Rodgers currently has the NFL's all-time regular season career passer rating record and is one of two quarterbacks to have a regular season career passer rating of over 100, the other being Russell Wilson. Rodgers is fifth all-time in postseason career passer rating, has the best touchdown-to-interception ratio in NFL history at 4.23, holds the league's lowest career interception percentage at 1.5 percent and the highest single-season passer rating record of 122.5. Due to the fact that Rodgers is the NFL's all-time regular season career passer rating leader, and his overall high level of play, Rodgers is considered by some sportscasters and players to be one of the greatest quarterbacks of all time

Aaron Rodgers is a great name for a baby boy or heck even a baby girl. A baby named after Aaron Rodgers could grow up to be one of the most accurate and mistake-free passers ever, with elite decision-making skills, a great arm, and exceptional mobility which all adds up to being one of the best players in football history.

Blake - is the first name of middle linebacker, Blake Martinez. Blake has been a tackling machine since entering the NFL in 2016. Martinez in 2017 had 144 tackles which was the most in the league, he was also a pro-bowl alternate the last two seasons.

Blake would be an awesome name for a baby boy. A baby named after Blake Martinez could grow up to tackle anything that comes his way and be a beast both in the weight room and om the football field.

Driver - is the last name of one of the all-time great receivers, Donald Driver. Donald holds the all-time packer receiving record for most 1,000 yard seasons, most receiving yards in a career, and most consecutive games with a reception. Not to mention Driver is a super bowl Champion and a Packer hall of famer.

Driver would be an amazing name for a baby boy. A baby named after Donald Driver could grow up to have track star jumping ability combined with football greatness. Also he probably would be a pretty damn good dancer too.

Chillar – is the last name of former linebacker, Brandon Chilar. Brandon was great at tackling, forcing fumbles and also was an instrumental part of the Packers Super bowl championship defense. Today Packer fans can find Brandon Chillar as one of the chief investors in the Elite Football league of India.

Chillar would be a nice name for a baby or girl. A baby named after Brandon Chillar could grow up to get tons of sacks in Dom Capers nickel defense, however might not be the best with money, i.e., see India Football league.

Clay – is the first name of Packer great, Clay Mathews. Clay is a six time pro bowler and the Defensive player of year in 2010. Clay Mathews is known for having a "motor that never stops" and is great at getting the big sack when it matters most.

Clay would be a remarkable name for a baby boy. A baby named after Clay Mathews aka the Claymaker, aka Big play Clay could grow up to have awesome biceps and Amazing hair not to mention the ability to turn the corner on any Offensive Tackle and end up in the quarterbacks face.

Collins - is the last name of Packers safety, Nick Collins. Nick was one of the best defense backs in Packer history. During his amazing career that was cut short by a neck injury, he was a three time pro bowler, NFL interception leader and Super Bowl champion.

Collins would be a great name for a baby boy. A baby named after Nick Collins could grow up to be a ball hawk that was always in the right place at the right time and always ready to make big plays on and off the field.

Finely - is the last name of Packers pro-bowl tight end, Jermichale Finely. Jermichale was a Packer from 2008 to 2013 before a neck injury ended his career. During his short playing career, Finely was one of the best pass catching tight ends in the game.

Finely would be a nice name for a baby boy. A baby named after Jermichale Finely could grow up to have amazing size and strength. He could be catching balls in the middle of the field all day long.

Flynn – is the last name of back-up quarterback, Matt Flynn. Matt held a clipboard most of his Packer career however one magical day in 2012 Flynn throw 6 touchdowns in one game.

Flynn would be a good name for a baby boy. A baby named after Matt Flynn may have one amazing game in his life which gets him payed the big bucks or he could bounce around from a bunch a different teams collecting pay checks. Either way he will make lots of money for doing very little.

Geronimo - is the first name of up and coming wide receiver Geronimo Allison. Geronimo was developing into one of Aaron Rodgers favorite targets before injury cut his season short.

Geronimo will be a decent name for a baby boy. A baby named after Geronimo Allison could grow up to have great size and speed and unlimited potential or they could be a fearless native American leader.

Grant – is the last name of Packers running back, Ryan Grant. Ryan Grant was a pro-bowl running back and Super bowl champion. He is best known by Packers fans for a huge playoff game against Seattle where he rushed for 206 yards and 3 touchdowns.

Grant would be a nice name for a baby boy. A baby named after Ryan Grant could grow up to be a reliable hard runner who could lead his team to a championship.

Hayward – is the last name of defensive back, Casey Hayward. Casey was a second round draft pick of the Packers in 2012 and ever since stepping foot on a NFL field has been able to be a ball-hawk / turn over machine. Hayward let the NFL in interceptions in 2016 and is a two time pro-bowler.

Hayward would be a great name for a baby boy. A baby named after Casey Hayward could grow up to be constantly in the "right place at the right time" and every time he turns around would be intercepting something.

Jackson – is the last name of packers 3rd down back, Brandon Jackson. Brandon was a dependable back-up to Ryan Grant and James Stark. He was also a key member to the Super Bowl 45 championship team.

Jackson would be an amazing name for a baby boy. A baby named after Brandon Jackson could grow up to be great at picking up blitzing linebackers and catching the ball in the flat on third down and two.

James Jones – is the first and last name of one of the most popular packers in the Aaron Rodgers era. Jones led the NFL in touchdowns in 2012 and was a big part of some of the most explosive offensives in league history.

James Jones would be a great name for a baby boy. A baby named after James could grow up to be a touchdown catching machine that is not only an asset to his football team but also his community.

Jordy - is the first name of one of the most loved player in Packer in history, Jordy Nelson. Jordy was also one of the best receivers in Packer history and for many years was one of the best "deep ball" threats in football. One could argue that Nelson was Aaron Rodgers favorite target and his 72 touchdown total could justify that.

Jordy would be an amazing name for a baby boy. A baby named after Jordy Nelson could grow up to be the kind of man that every father wants his daughter to marry. Some who has awesome character and integrity on and off the football field.

Kapri – is the first name of little known running back Kapri Bibbs, Kapri came to the Packers midseason in 2018 and has been a third string running back who only saw the field from the sidelines for most of the year. The good news is he has a really great name.

Kapri would be a great name for a baby girl. A baby named after Kapri Bibbs could grow up to have a unique name and be unknown for their football skills

Kingsley – is the first name of Packers D-lineman Kingsley Keke. Kingsley has yet to play a snap during the writing of this book. He is a very promising rookie and has a great name.

Kingsley would be an awesome baby boy's name. A baby named after Kingsley Keke could grow up to be big fast and strong, which is always a good thing.

Kumerow - is the last name of Packers fan favorite receive, Jake Kumerow. Jake was a UW- Whitewater legend and what little time he has had with the Packers he has not disappointed.

Kumerow would be an amazing name for a baby boy or girl. A baby named after Jake Kumerow could grow up to have deep ball speed with great hair.

Lane - is the first name of Offensive lineman, Lane Taylor. Lane was signed by the Packers as a undrafted free agent in 2013 and has been able to improve his skills each year to become a dependable starter.

Lane would be a nice name for a baby boy or girl. A baby named after Lane Taylor could grow up to be someone that is able to overcome long odds to become a starter in the NFL.

Lang - is the last name of Packers Guard, T.J. Lang. T.J was part of the Super Bowl 45 team and during that time was one of the best guards in all of football, earning two pro bowl appearances.

Lang would be a good name for a baby boy. A baby name after T.J Lang could grow up to be a large man with great foot work and the ability to protect his friend baby Aaron Rodgers,

Lattimore – is the last name of Linebacker, Jamari Lattimore. Jamari was a steady force on both special team and rushing the quarterback during 2011-2014 season.

Lattimore would be an amazing name for a baby boy. A baby named after Jamari Lattimore could grow up to be big, fast and feared by quarterbacks.

Linsley - is the last name of Packers center, Corey Linsley. Corey has been one of the most consistent offensive lineman in the NFL since being drafted in 2014. Linsley is known for his quick feet and ability to read the defense and call out switches to his fellow O-lineman.

Linsley would be an good name for a baby girl. A baby named after Corey Linsley could grow up to be a very dependable and critical part of a team who is a major asset to not only their team but also their community.

Marcedes – is the first name of veteran tight end Marcedes Lewis. Marcedes has been a Packer at the tail end of his career and does not see much playing time, However in his prime he was one of the best tight ends in football and was a pro- bowler in 2010.

Marcedes would be a great name for a baby boy or girl. A baby named after Mercedes Lewis could grow up to be a huge target in the red zone and an awesome blocker.

Mason – is the first name of Packers all-time scoring leader, Mason Crosby. Mason has been the Packers kicker since 2007 and during that time has been one of the best in the NFL. Mason is a Super bowl champion and future Packer hall of famer.

Mason would be an awesome name for a baby boy. A baby boy named after Mason Crosby could grow up to be a clutch kicker who could make the game winning field goal with three seconds left on the clock.

Starks - is the last name of running back James Starks. James was a 6th round draft by the Packers in 2010. As a rookie James contributed greatly to winning Super Bowl 45 and holds a number of rookie playoff rushing records for his performance that year. In the years after the Super Bowl Starks was a powerful rusher with great hands out of the backfield.

Starks would be as great name for a baby boy. A baby named after James Starks could grow up to be a great down-hill runner who comes up big in important games.

Woodson – is the last name of Packers all-time great, Charles Woodson. Charles was a 9 time pro-bowler along with being named defensive player of the year in 2009. Woodson is a member of the NFL 2000's all-decade team and is soon to be in both The Packers and pro football hall of fames.

Woodson would be an amazing name for a baby boy. A baby name after Charles Woodson could grow up to be a national college champion and a super bowl champ. He would also be awesome at the Heisman pose too.

Names to Avoid

Bostick – is the last name of former Packer Brandon Bostick. Brandon was a third string tight end who claim to shame is misplaying the ball on the onside kick in the 2014 NFC championship game which contributed to the packers lost. I know the lost was not all his fault but he is a good place to start. No one wants a baby whose name will bring back the memory of that horrible game over and over again.

Bulaga – is the last name of Offensive Lineman, Bryan Bulaga. Bryan, when healthy is one of the better offensive tackles in the game. He was also the youngest person to start in a super bowl. A baby Bulaga sounds like a whale and unless you think your baby is going to be massive in size, this name should be avoided.

Clinton-Dixs - is the last name of former Packers number one draft pick HaHa Clinton Dixs. HaHa had a very up and down packer career. However everyone especially in Washington D. C. knows you always stay away from a Clinton-Dix just ask Monica Lewinski (easy joke). Just avoid this name for your new baby.

Crabtree – is the last name of tight end, Tom Crabtree. Tom was a back-up for all of his career and ended up with two touchdowns. If your baby is a little Crabtree you can expect a lot of crying so avoid this name. Maybe pick happy tree or maybe avoid a name with tree in it all together

Equanimeous – is the first name of the Packers up and coming wide receiver Equanimeous St. Brown. This name should be avoided due to the fact it's hard to say and even harder to spell. I think Mr. St Brown is safe being the only Equanimeous in Green Bay.

Guian - is the last name of Packer Lineman, Letroy Guian. Letroy was had 8.5 sacks and 180 total sacks in his 8 year NFL career however he was most known for the amount of food he could put down and the weed he smoked. This name should be avoided at all cost, after all parents wants to show off their cute little guy not their cute little Guian.

Harrell – is the last name of the Packers first round draft pick, Justin Harrell. Justin was supposed to be the next great pass rushing, quarterbacking sacking stud for the Packers. However he ended up only getting 28 total tackles and 0 sacks in 4 seasons. Harrell should be avoided as a baby name since you don't want your baby to be injured all the time that never lives up to expectations.

Johnny Jolly – is the first and last name of former Packer Defensive lineman, Johnny Jolly. Though he seems like a happy guy with a big smile, he just could not stay out of legal trouble. A baby named after Johnny Jolly could grow up loving purple drink and codeine which is not a good thing, so just avoid this name.

Lumpkin - is the last name of Packers back up running back Kregg Lumpkin. Kregg played two years for the Packers and was really only known because his named rhymes with pumpkin. Yes the Packers had a Lumpkin Pumpkin at their guest relations guest. Lumpkin could be a cute nickname for baby but being named Lumpkin in middle school could be painful.

Schum - is the last name of Packers punter, Jake Schum. The first rule of naming a baby is never name them after a Punter. The second is don't name them Schum.

Sitton - is the last name of one of Aaron Rodgers protectors, Josh Sitton. Josh was a one of the best guards in football from 2012 to 2016. Though Josh Sitton was an amazing football player no parent wants to introduce their little Sitton to the family. A Sitton should be something baby does in their diaper not what they learn to write in Kindergarten.

Spitz - is the last name of former guard, Jason Spitz. Jason was a solid player from 2006-2010, however let's face it no one in their right mind is going to name their baby Spitz. So skip this name and maybe go with his first name Jason.

Final Thought's

Parents have the duty to give their child a good name, (hopefully a Packer name), however your job as a parent does not end when it is printed on a birth certificate. In Fact, the act of being a parent never ends and should be the most important and rewarding part of your life regardless of your child's name.

Remember overall a baby's name doesn't matter, what does is that your new bundle of joy, get genuine, unconditional love. Always keep in mind a child with good parenting rarely fails in life!

Bibliography

"Birth of a Team and a Legend". Green Bay Packers. Archived from the original on February 18, 2014. Retrieved December 12, 2016.

^ "Club Information" (PDF). 2019 Green Bay Packers Media Guide. NFL Enterprises, LLC. July 30, 2019. Retrieved September 4, 2019.

^ "Green Bay Packers Team Capsule" (PDF). 2018 Official National Football League Record and Fact Book. NFL Enterprises, LLC. August 9, 2018. Retrieved August 14, 2018.

^ Jump up to:ᵃ ᵇ "Shareholders". Packers.com. NFL Enterprises, LLC. Retrieved January 22, 2015.

^ "Birth of a Team, and a Legend" (PDF). 2018 Green Bay Packers Media Guide. NFL Enterprises, LLC. September 12, 2018. Retrieved May 8, 2019.

^ Jump up to:ᵃ ᵇ Names, Larry D (1987). "The Myth". In Scott, Greg (ed.). The History of the Green Bay Packers: The Lambeau Years. 1. Angel Press of WI. p. 30. ISBN 0-939995-00-X.

^ "Chronology of Professional Football" (PDF). National Football League. January 22, 2015. Retrieved January 22, 2015.

^ "Green Bay Packers Team History". Pro Football Hall of Fame. Retrieved February 24, 2016.

^ Jump up to:ᵃ ᵇ *Zirin, Dave (January 25, 2011). "Those Non-Profit Packers". The New Yorker. Retrieved December 28, 2014.*

^ Jump up to:ᵃ ᵇ *"Super Bowls & Championships". Green Bay Packers. Retrieved December 12, 2016.*

^ {{cite web|url=https://www.pro-football-reference.com/teams/gnb/

^ *"The Acme Packers were short-lived". packers.com. Retrieved August 1, 2018.*

^ *"A name 90 years in the making". archive.jsonline.com. Retrieved August 1, 2018.*

^ *"The truth and myth about 'The Hungry Five'". packers.com. Retrieved August 1, 2018.*

^ *"Dec. 8, 1929: Packers earn first league title". Retrieved August 1, 2018.*

^ *"History of Champions: Packers are No. 1 in NFL". Press Gazette Media. Retrieved August 1, 2018.*

^ *"Team Records: Games Won" (PDF). National Football League. Retrieved December 12,2016.*

^ *"Don Hutson: Information from". Answers.com. Retrieved February 7, 2011.*

^ *Fleming, David (September 27, 2013). "Blaze of Glory". ESPN. Retrieved December 9,2014.*

^ *Maraniss, David (September 14, 1999). "In throes of winter, a team in disarry is reborn". Milwaukee Journal Sentinel. Milwaukee, Wisconsin. p. 2B. Retrieved July 6, 2011.*

^ *Pennington, Bill (January 16, 2008). "NYTimes article of January 15, 2008". The New York Times. Retrieved February 7, 2011.*

^ *"Vince Lombardi Record, Statistics, and Category Ranks | Pro-Football-Reference.com"*. *Pro-Football-Reference.com*. *Retrieved August 1, 2018.*

^ *"AP Was There: 1967 Cowboys-Packers Ice Bowl game"*. *USA Today. Retrieved August 1, 2018.*

^ *"The 100 Greatest Moments in Sports History | The Ice Bowl"*. *Sports Illustrated's 100 Greatest Moments. Retrieved August 1, 2018.*

^ Old School Packers Archived February 18, 2006, at the Wayback Machine from the Milwaukee Journal Sentinel website. Retrieved February 5, 2007

Printed in the United States
by Baker & Taylor Publisher Services